Pure Love

Jason Evert

D0731642

2018

Pure Love
Jason Evert
©2018, Chastity Project
Third Edition

Published by Chastity Project
PO Box 5065
Scottsdale, AZ 85261
www.chastityproject.org

Cover by Devin Schadt
Interior design by Russell Design

Printed in the United States of America
ISBN 978-0-9894905-0-4

If you're like me, you've been told that sex is bad. But when you ask why, you hear something like, "It's just bad, so don't do it," or "You'll get a disease or get pregnant!" While I'm sure you realize that sex has its consequences—and they might be bad if they happen—these reasons aren't always convincing.

Our generation has been taught how to avoid venereal infections, but what we really want to know is how to find, build, and maintain a relationship of real love. Sex is supposed to be a great gift, so it's easy to get tired of hearing about the diseases and unwed pregnancy rates. If you're ready for a different approach, and you want the gift of sex to be as great as it was meant to be, read on.

"How do I find love?"

Everyone wants love. Everyone longs to give himself or herself to another. We're made for love, and that need in us is so deep that many would rather risk getting pregnant or getting an STD than live without love. We may be willing to take these risks because the world tells us that sex means "making love." Then we see relationships in which sex destroyed love, and we wonder what went wrong.

Some people claim that they choose to be sexually active simply to have fun or be accepted by others. But these same people often end up wondering why the "fun" involved so much disappointment and why their quest for acceptance left them feeling more alone than ever. The only solution capable of breaking through this hurt and confusion is the virtue known as chastity.

"What's chastity?"

Chastity is a virtue (like courage or honesty) that applies to a person's sexuality. It means that you order your sexual desires according to the demands of real love. For example, when you love a person, you do whatever is necessary to keep from harming them, and you're willing to make heroic sacrifices in order to do what is best for them. Chastity means that you take this definition of love and apply it to sex.

Some think that chastity simply means "no sex." But that's abstinence: focusing on what you can't do and can't have. Chastity focuses on what you can do and can have, right now: a lifestyle that brings freedom, respect, peace, and even romance—without regret.

Because chastity involves purity and self-control, some people think it means sexual repression. On the contrary, it frees a couple from the selfish attitude of using each other as objects, thus making them capable of true love.

"How do you know when it's love?"

You can never judge the value of a relationship by the intensity of the feelings, because these will always come and go. Feeling in love is exciting, but emotions should never be confused with love. For example, a young man might have genuine feelings for girl, but this does not guarantee that he loves her. The real measure of love is to do what's best for the beloved. Sure, this is demanding. That's why true love is so rare, and that's what makes it so beautiful and worth it.

The opposite of loving is using. For example, guys often use girls for physical gratification, and girls may use guys for social or emotional gratification. But, they're never satisfied. I've spoken to more than a million high school and college students, and I've never met a girl who longed for a series of physical relationships. But I've met countless discouraged young women who were trying to find love by doing just this. Maybe they were confusing physical affection with love, or were looking for some affirmation of their worth that their dads never gave them. Either way, these girls weren't finding what they wanted.

Likewise, I've met "players" who said they longed to know how to love women instead of destroying them. They didn't intend to harm girls, but no one ever showed them—or expected them—to treat women with reverence. Dissatisfied with the lifestyle of "getting some," they realized that to sexually conquer a woman was to miss the point of being a man. Only with the fullest giving of themselves in authentic love will they ever find themselves.

If you're sexually active and trying to figure out if it's love, apply the love test. Take the sexual part out of the relationship and live the virtue of chastity. When you remove the lust, you can see if there was ever any love to begin with. Don't be afraid to do this, because *only when love is put to the test can its real value be seen.*

"What if we really love each other?"

If you really love each other, then you'll do what's best for your relationship. However, 80 percent of the time, the physical intimacy of a teen's first sexual relationship won't last more than six months.[1] A couple might think that the statistics wouldn't apply to them because they care so much about each other. But if a guy is sleeping with a woman who is not his wife, is he really doing what is best for her? If he is, then why would he jump out her bedroom window if he heard her dad's footsteps coming down the hall? It's because he knows that their mutual feelings of admiration and attraction do not make their sexual activity an act of love.

Once sex enters the picture, it often becomes the relationship's center, forcing everything else aside. Both people become objects to be used instead of persons to be loved, even though they may do not intend this, and rarely admit to seeing each other that way. One college student admitted, "I thought sex was going to make us so much closer as a couple. But before long, he didn't want to spend time with *me* any more—he wanted to spend time with *my body*. Looking back, I now realize that I wasn't in love with him. I was in love with the feeling of being wanted by someone."

Your body is a gift, and during the sexual act, the couple give themselves to each other. But to reduce this gift to a loan gives you less respect than you deserve. That's why the total gift of one's body and heart belongs in a permanent and faithful relationship: marriage. We might feel like we're more "in love" than some married people, but emotions don't create a marriage, and they can't hold one together.

Also, you can't truly give yourself unless you realize your worth and the magnitude of the gift you're exchanging. True love says, "You are everything to me. I give myself totally to you forever." This is the real commitment that springs from the heart of every person who is sincerely in love. It demands permanence, not just hooking-up. It does not insist on its own way when desires are strong, and it can sacrifice the desires of the moment for something permanent. After all, if you can't say "no" to sex, then what is your "yes" worth?

"How can it be wrong if no one gets hurt?"

Although it may be hard to see now, sex outside of marriage hurts both people. Besides the obvious risks of disease and unwanted pregnancy, it scars you emotionally. One husband admitted, "I would do anything—*anything*—to forget the sexual experiences I had before I met my wife. . . . The pictures of the other women from my past go through my head, and it's killing any intimacy. The truth is that I've been married to this wonderful woman for eight years and I have never been 'alone' in the bedroom with her."[2] If and when you get married, the sexual experiences you've had with others may weigh upon the heart of your future spouse, not to mention the spouse of the person you're dating. This obviously isn't good for any marriage.

Even if a couple doesn't think that anyone is getting hurt, they may be using sex to cover up problems and making things worse. When this happens, one gynecologist said, "Many teenagers feel that something is wrong—not with sex itself, but with themselves. So, they try harder to make sex 'work,' to make sex provide those things they think it should: intimacy, love, trust, acceptance, appreciation of their masculinity or femininity, relief from their loneliness. When it doesn't work, millions of teenagers . . . turn their anger and hurt inward, resulting in depression. . . . We repeatedly return to certain behaviors such as sex, drugs, or drinking to get something that continually eludes us."[3]

Also, sex outside of marriage usually hurts our relationship with our parents because that lifestyle is often accompanied by lies. Gossip usually follows at school, and otherwise lasting friendships are sometimes sacrificed for a date who doesn't last. One high school girl emailed me, saying, "I have lost friends, but most of all I have lost myself. I feel as if I am unlovable; therefore the only type of love I can receive is fake sexual love. Anyone around me would think I'm just a happy normal teenager, but if everything were so good, I wouldn't be crying at night."

So, a better question to ask is this: Who *isn't* hurt by premarital sex? This may all be difficult to see right now, because it's tough to see beyond the circle of your friends and the walls of your school. But it's wise to not make any life-changing decisions based on the opinions of classmates, most of whom you'll never see again after graduation.

"What if we're both okay with it?"

Ever hear a girl say the following: "I'm seeing this guy my friends and family hate. They say he's possessive, but that's the way he shows how much he cares. I started having sex with him because I really care about him, too. Why can't people see how great he is?"

While this girl thinks the problem is that people dislike her boyfriend, the real problem is that she can't see *why*. Once sex enters the picture, it is almost impossible to be objective about a relationship. This is partly because of what sex does to your mind. During sexual arousal, the brain releases a hormone called oxytocin.[4] It works like human superglue because it causes a great emotional bond, increases trust, and makes you less critical of the other person.[5]

Such blinding and binding helps married couples to persevere through tough times. But outside of marriage it can be dangerous. For example, because oxytocin influences you to focus on the positive aspects and memories of the person, it is easier to overlook the risks of a relationship. One scientist noted, "Oxytocin may affect the extent of these negative evaluations, causing us to say, 'Oh, this won't be too bad.'"[6] Research also shows that intense bonding deactivates the circuits in the brain that are supposed to make judgments about another person![7] This may explain why some people stay in dead-end relationships even though their friends keep warning them to get out. Since estrogen increases the oxytocin response, females experience more intense bonding than men, and suffer more from broken bonds.[8]

So, when a relationship ends—especially if it is sexual—the couple may feel as if they're experiencing an emotional divorce. In basic terms, sharing the gift of sex is like putting a piece of tape on someone's arm. The first bond is strong, and it will be painful if removed. But if you put the same tape on another's arm, it will be easier to remove. Each time the tape is removed, the bond is weakened because of the leftover residue on the tape. The same is true in relationships, where previous sexual experiences may interfere with the ability to bond. However, by practicing purity (or starting over if you've made mistakes in the past), you prepare yourself for a greater bond with your future spouse.

So, why does sex belong only in marriage? One obvious explanation is that sex makes children, and children belong in families. But there is an even more profound reason, stamped into our own hearts (and bodies): just as people speak a language with their words, they also speak a language with their body. In sex, the body is saying, "I give myself entirely to you. There's nothing of me that I'm not giving you." But if the couple is not married, then they're speaking a lie with their bodies. They're saying, "I give you my body (but I won't give you myself)." Or, "I'm totally yours (until I'm totally someone else's)." In sex, the body makes a promise, even if you won't. So, sex belongs in marriage because only then do the bodies speak the truth: I am yours.

"But what's wrong with sex if the relationship leads to marriage?"

If you hope to marry someone, you obviously want the relationship to last. But are you willing to do what it takes to save your marriage before it starts? Consider this: If a guy gets married as a virgin, his divorce rate is 63 percent lower than a non-virgin. For girls, it's 76 percent lower.[9] There could be several reasons why virgins have lower divorce rates. One reason, according to the journal *Adolescent and Family Health*, is that "Those who have premarital sex are more likely to have extramarital sex (affairs)—and extramarital sex contributes to many divorces."[10]

Perhaps a more common reason for the divorce connection is that many sexually active couples make bad marriage decisions because lust causes a false sense of unity. The passion forfeits their ability to look clearly at each other as potential spouses, and the lust can cover up an absence of true love, which never developed. Some couples don't intend to use each other, but want to live together or have sex to feel close to each other. However, couples who live together before marriage have a divorce rate nearly 80 percent higher than those who waited until after the wedding to move in together.[11] They're also more than three times as likely to experience infidelity.[12]

If you're going to get married, you'll have the rest of your lives to enjoy sexual intimacy. But now is the only time you'll ever have to prepare for marriage. Consider what makes marriages last: patience, self-control, and sacrifice. Now consider the qualities an abstinent dating couple has to practice: patience, self-control, and sacrifice. When pleasure is valued more than these qualities, couples miss the chance to build the virtues that make love last. After all, being united for life is better than feeling united for a few nights. The fact is: *mutual sacrifice intensifies love*; refusing to sacrifice extinguishes it.

"Is other stuff okay, as long as we don't have sex?"

I know a woman whom I'll call Kate. Her friends were sexually active, so she figured that as long as she kept her virginity, she was good. Kate's boyfriend said that he respected her commitment to virginity, telling her, "I don't want to pressure you to do anything you're not ready for." This made her think that he was a gentleman, and that he loved her. However, he made her feel that she owed him other sexual favors, since she was "holding out" on him. Her girlfriends reminded her that guys have sexual "needs," and that if she wanted to keep him, she'd have to give him something.

Little by little, Kate gave him everything he wanted: except her virginity. She reminded herself that her friends were doing worse things, but she knew she was being used.

Years later, she married someone else and regretted giving in to her ex-boyfriend. Even though she hadn't technically had sex with him, the bond was there, and so were the regrets. This is the bitter fruit that comes by comparing ourselves with those in worse relationships. To avoid this, set a higher standard, because you'll get what you'll settle for. Doing so will spare your heart many wounds. Treat your body as a gift to be guarded jealously, a gift that can be given only with a wedding ring and the lifelong commitment of true love that comes with it.

We always hear about "experimenting" with our sexuality, but you don't "experiment" with something priceless. You experiment with things of little worth that are easily replaced. So, when we experiment with our hearts and the gift of our bodies, we begin to value them less and less.

"Isn't everybody doing it?"
No. Countless young people have realized the truth about what love is and what sex is worth. They've had their fill of what MTV and *Cosmo* are saying, and they won't be robbed of their chance to have the love they've always wanted.

Contrary to what the media portrays, teen sexual activity rates have been dropping for over a decade, and now the majority of high school students are virgins.[13] In fact, research shows that the sexual activity rate of high school boys has been dropping twice as quickly as that of high school girls![14] Among those who have already lost their virginity, two-thirds of them wished they had waited longer to have sex (77 percent of girls and 60 percent of guys).[15] But, because of social pressure, even those who are virgins often pretend that they're not. This gives people the impression that everyone is doing it, even though the majority isn't. The pressure also leads some to think of virginity as an embarrassment rather than a gift. But think about it: if your future spouse waited all his or her life to give that gift to you alone, would you feel embarrassed for them, or honored?

"Who would want to save sex for marriage?"

- NFL Quarterback Philip Rivers saved his virginity for marriage, and explained, "It's the greatest gift you could give your wife."[16]
- Former NBA all-star A. C. Green was also married as a virgin. Before meeting his wife, he said, "I have respect for myself and the women I've dated. I try not to focus on idle thoughts that can turn to temptations. . . . I know there's something better for me if I wait."[17] Now married, he adds, "It is definitely worth waiting. When you marry the right person at the right time you have no regrets. For me, I have nothing but smiles on my face. . . . The first year with the Laker team my rookie season, they took bets out." He recalls team-

mates telling him, "There's no way you will be talking abstinence, no way you'll remain a virgin. None of that's possible. Once you see what's going inside the NBA, in the league, you will do everything because these girls are beautiful." Even today, he says, "Most of the guys have come back . . . [and] now they are saying, 'You know what, I sort of wish I had rethought some of my decisions. I wouldn't be in this situation now.'[18]

- Christie, a high school senior, said this about her potential spouse: "His abstinence from sex is one way to prove his ability to be true to me. I would be so honored to find out that the man I want to marry has respected me enough—without even knowing me—not to have sex with anyone else but me."

- Michael, a twenty-three-year-old, said, "I've had the opportunity to give away my virginity a few times, but I kept thinking about my future wife. Some people during high school joked about it, but I'm so happy I took the path that I did. When I lift my wife's veil on our wedding day, who will be laughing then?"

- "I came inches away from losing my virginity at the age of fourteen, on a dark football field, with a guy I barely knew," said a college junior. "I don't know how it happened. I had always been so strong. Then somehow there I was, about to give away my most real possession. I had the courage to stop, and since that day I've worn a ring to hold the place where my wedding band will go, to remind me of the gift I am saving for my husband."

The more innocence you save, the greater your joy will be to share it all on the wedding night. Some disagree, and say that sex is meant for fun. But if that's the case, why do surveys of over 100,000 people reveal that married couples who enter marriage with little or no sexual history—have the most satisfying sex lives?[19] If you think sleeping around will prepare you to be a better spouse, the evidence says the opposite.[20]

One young woman said, "I thought I was ready for sex because I felt so in love. It was all based on emotions, and I thought sex would be the way to keep him. But once the relationship ended, sex didn't seem like a big deal. I was 'living in the moment,' and didn't see—or want to admit—what I was doing to myself. Now, years later, I'll be married soon and I wish more than anything that I had waited."

Your virginity was never meant to be "lost," as if it had been misplaced somewhere. It's meant to be given as a gift to the one who deserves it: your spouse. Even if you've lost your virginity, and think this doesn't apply to you, read on. It's never too late.

"What if I'm not a virgin?"
While the loss of virginity has to do with the past,

chastity has to do with today. Regardless of what happened last week or last year, you are still worth waiting for. Maybe you lost your virginity, or maybe it was taken from you. Either way, you still have yourself to give. Beginning today, pursue a life of purity.

It's never too late to regain your purity, but the process is challenging. Sometimes it's easy to end bad relationships, but it's tough to keep from jumping back into them. Unfortunately, many who feel like they've given everything away wonder if they have anything left to give. Instead of starting over, they bury one mistake under another so the original wounds won't look so bad. They run from one physical relationship to another, thinking that pleasure will fill their need for love. But this makes the healing process more difficult.

"After I lost my virginity," Crystal confessed, "I didn't respect myself, and one empty relationship led to another. Ever since I was a little girl, I wanted the perfect love, but after all I had done I thought I was the last person on earth to deserve it. Eventually, I realized that finding a good guy wasn't a matter of luck. I started over, raised my standards, and made a commitment to chastity. Now, three years later—and engaged—I haven't regretted a day since."

I remember meeting one girl who slept with fifteen guys in three months. Her school labeled her a slut. When I asked her why she did this, she said, "Well, it's fun—going to parties and hooking up." I asked her if it really was fun. With tears in her eyes, she answered, "No, it's not fun. My parents are getting divorced, and there's so much hurt and hate in my family. And just for a minute, when those guys hold me, it feels like love. I know it's not, but at least I feel like somebody wants me." This is not a slut. This is a woman with a heart identical to yours and mine, longing for love.

How do you get out of this lifestyle? Well, what advice would you give to your future spouse if right now he or she were sleeping with someone you'll never meet? Follow that same advice, and you'll make it.

In your heart, forgive those who have hurt you, and forgive yourself. We all have things in our past that we wish we could erase. But, by practicing chastity in future relationships, you'll see that *living purity will heal the past*. In the meantime, don't assume you always need to be in a relationship. Independence and maturity are attractive qualities.

As a reminder of your commitment and new lifestyle, you could buy a white candle. If you choose to get married one day, you could let your spouse light it on your wedding night.

"If we aren't going to have sex, how far can we go?"

If you're going to get married one day, perhaps someone right now is dating the person you'll eventually marry. How far is too far for them? Practice the purity you would hope your future spouse would have, and treat your dates with the respect that you hope your future spouse would be given. Or, consider how you'll expect a guy to treat your daughter one day. By listening to your conscience, you'll know where to draw the line. When we ignore that voice in our heart that tells us right from wrong and give in for the sake of excitement, we end up feeling empty afterward.

So, "How far is too far?" is the wrong question. While driving, would you see how close you could come to hitting oncoming traffic? By the time you find out how far is too far, it would be too late. In the same way, we shouldn't ask, "How far can we go before doing something we'll really regret?" Instead, think, "How far can we go toward purity?" Perhaps such an idea strikes you as extreme, oppressive, or simply boring. If so, realize that chastity isn't a burden or a list of rules. It's a change of heart: from "getting some" to giving all. In fact, the more responsible you feel for your beloved, the more true love there is.

Sexual passion is supposed to be a good thing. However, igniting sexual passion outside of marriage is like taking fire out of the fireplace and putting it in the living room. Even a good thing can become destructive if it's used in the wrong way. Once the flame of sexual desire is ignited, it's like a fire that doesn't stop burning until everything in its path is consumed. Previous intimacies may become old and the boundaries are often pushed back to find more excitement and closeness. The couple may even depend on pleasure in order to feel close, and before long, all that may be left is sex. In the long run, their impatient desire for oneness robs them of the opportunity to grow in love, and thus to experience true joy.

When a couple is pure, they still desire to be one. But because of their standards, they choose to channel those powerful desires into creative ways of expressing love. As a result, their friendship and intimacy deepens, and the relationship becomes stronger.

Some people say, "Saving sexual arousal for marriage is too old-fashioned and unrealistic. You need to hook up with at east a few people so you'll have sexual experience. That way, you'll be a greater gift for your spouse on your wedding night." Regardless of a person's sexual history (or lack thereof), we are all worthy of love. But who hopes that their future spouse will amass sexual experiences in order to become a greater gift? Odds are, you would rather your future spouse save his or her first kiss for you. If you would treasure that gift of innocence, why not begin to value your purity as well?

So abstinence isn't just the absence of sex, it's the expression of love. In fact, as a single person, abstinence is a greater expression of love than making love itself, because you're doing what's best for the other person. What was once seen as just "waiting" becomes a time of formation that teaches you how to love. With chastity, even if you aren't dating someone, you can prepare for your future spouse right now by training yourself in faithfulness.

"What if I want to be free to do whatever I want?"

You want freedom? How about no longer worrying about questions like "Will I get a disease? Will my parents find out? Will we get pregnant? Am I being used?" Freed from these problems, you'll be free to love—without anxiety about the future or regrets about the past. This is true freedom: the ability to do what's right.

You're right to desire freedom, because freedom makes love possible. But realize that chastity isn't the loss of freedom; it's the fulfillment of it. A person who is controlled by his hormones is not free. He isn't giving himself to a woman or loving her, but using her as an outlet for his sexual "needs." While lust blinds us and distorts our desires, purity liberates us. After all, you don't become free by doing whatever you want. You become free—and able to love—when you have self-control.

"Won't chastity ruin the excitement of dating?"

Not in the least. Chastity does away with the mind

games often played to get someone into bed. Sadly, many women give sex to men for the sake of getting "love," while the men often seem to give "love" for the sake of getting sex. Your heart—and the gift of sex—is made for something better than that.

After all, giving in to one's hormones is not romance. This is lust, and while it may be spontaneous and temporarily exciting, using another person isn't romantic. In fact, too many good, romantic relationships have been ruined by lust.

Sometimes a person's actions may appear romantic because they're so imaginative and thoughtful, but the actions may be done to manipulate or seduce the other. This is not romance because love is absent. Only when purity is present can one tell the difference between loving romance and selfish seduction. If you inform your date that you won't sleep with him or her, and that person leaves you—then you know immediately what you were being "loved" for. If you're looking for excitement, knowing that you're loved is much more exciting than wondering if you're being used.

So, purity doesn't mean being a prude. It means that you have the strength to conquer lust so that you're free to fall in love for the right reasons. Purity doesn't mean you have a negative or unhealthy view of sex. You just know how much it's worth, and you realize that *if you give it away for free, you're saying that it isn't worth anything*. In the words of one woman, "when you put on chastity, you'll discover a life more hope-filled, more vibrant, more *real* than anything you might have experienced while having sex outside of marriage. *That* is the thrill of the chaste."[21]

"What about pornography? I'm not hurting anyone."

Pornography trains people to measure the value of others based upon how much lust we feel for them. We may jokingly try to convince ourselves that it isn't a problem, but our ability to love is being crippled. While we're busy fantasizing, our masculinity and femininity becomes warped, and if we enter into real relationships, we'll make the frustrating mistake of confusing love with lust. While love involves sacrifice and commitment, pornography teaches us to reduce others to sexual objects that can be used and then discarded once our passion wears off. We're made for love, but we can't love a fantasy and it can't love us.

Although pornography isn't just a male problem, consider how it affects men: when a man loves a woman, he loves her for who she is. Such love is impossible with pornography because the man "loves" only what she gives him. He has no idea who the woman is. That's why it has been said that the problem with pornography is not that it shows too *much*, but that it shows too *little*. It shows too little because it reduces a woman to her body parts. Instead of inviting you to manhood, pornography trains you to reject responsibility for a woman. Referring to web sites and magazines as "adult" or to a strip joint as a "gentleman's club" couldn't be further from the truth. Women know that real men don't indulge in either. After all, what kind of guy needs to pay money so that a woman pretends that she likes him?

Some argue that porn is just a harmless way to relieve temptations. But pornography doesn't get rid of temptations any more than prostitution does. Besides, our goal isn't to get rid of sexual desire but to master our desires for the sake of love. The idea that pornography can be used to decrease temptation is like saying that lighter fluid can be used to extinguish a fire. Just as purity teaches you to give, porn teaches you to take. It incites lustful thoughts, and leads you to believe that you deserve—and need—sexual gratification whenever the desires arise. However, nothing bad happens to a man's body if he isn't sexually active.

Love is a gift of self, but you cannot give what you do not possess. So, if you don't have self-control, you can't truly give yourself to another. If a person can't conquer his habit of lust, then how will he love a spouse one day? Instead of using his fantasies for sexual gratification, he'll use his wife.

In fact, *pornography is the perfect way to ruin your future marriage.* It trains the brain to associate sex with dirty, illicit, sexual fantasies of countless disposable women. And, even though it takes only a few seconds to see the pictures, it takes years to forget them. This causes tremendous strain in marriage, because the spouse is compared to the models and is expected to provide as much excitement. When this doesn't happen, the couple suffers and the spouse feels hurt and unable to "live up" to the fantasies. Who wants to put his or her future spouse through this?

Pornography also trains a person to get bored with commitment. For example, no matter how perfect a model might be, the man hooked on porn will leave her behind within a matter of seconds in order to view others. To the extent a man entrenches himself in the habit of viewing porn, he robs himself of the ability to be captivated by a woman.

In the words of one husband, pornography causes "those distortions of our sexual desires that we must struggle *against* in order to discover true love."[22] So, if you own pornography, for the love of your future spouse, trash it *immediately.* To the degree you love women, fight pornography.

"What about safe sex?"

There is no such thing. In fact, the very concept of

"safe sex" is degrading. For one, it equates us with animals that need to be neutered because they have no self-control. Secondly, it reduces human sexuality to a merely genital act because it implies that people are is "safe" as long as they don't get pregnant or infected. What about a person's emotions, future relationships, reputation, and family life? All of this is impacted by sexual activity, but seems to be ignored by those who call sex with a condom "safe." Shouldn't we be concerned about protecting the entire person, instead of just the reproductive organs? Finally, contraceptive sex gives people a license to use others by enjoying the pleasures of sex without permanent commitment. By encouraging people to be "protected" instead of respected, those who support safe sex are causing the problems they pretend to solve. For example, here are the statistics you never hear:

- Human papillomavirus (HPV) is the most common STD in the world.[23] It causes 99.7 percent of cervical cancer,[24] and this kills more than 288,000 women each year![25] So, with each sexual partner a woman has, her risk of cervical cancer increases. Your body, like your heart, isn't made for multiple sexual partners. It's made for enduring love.
- While condom use may reduce the risk of HPV-related diseases, it doesn't offer adequate protection from

HPV, because the virus is spread from skin-to-skin contact throughout the entire genital area, including one's thighs and lower abdomen.[26] How common is it? The Centers for Disease Control reported that *the majority of sexually active women have been infected with one or more types of genital HPV.*[27] Good luck finding *that* on the warning label of a condom!

- If you have sex with a person, you're basically having sex with everyone that they've had sex with, not to mention the others their partners have had sex with. By having sexual contact with one person, you could be exposing yourself to the STDs of hundreds of people.[28] This is frightening, considering that 80 percent of people who have an STD are unaware of their own infection.[29] For example, a person who has the HIV virus may not show symptoms of AIDS for up to ten years.

- Oral sex can transmit virtually every STD,[30] and hand-to-genital contact can transmit some as well.[31] So, even virgins can get STDs,[32] including oral cancer from HPV.[33]

- If a woman gets chlamydia and isn't treated in time, she may become infertile. Seventy-five percent of women (and 50 percent of men) don't show symptoms after they contract it.[34] Thus, it is called "the silent sterilizer." *Think, girls: Is this guy worth losing your ability to ever have kids?*

- Most STDs can be carried into marriage undetected. For example, 90 percent of people with genital herpes do not know that they are infected.[35] In the case of HPV, it will often clear on its own. But when a husband is infected with it, his wife is five times as likely to get cervical cancer.[36]
- Several STDs are incurable, and many can be passed on from a mother to her baby. For the newborn, this can cause brain damage, blindness, deafness, pneumonia, liver disease, and even death.
- One out of every six teenage girls will become pregnant during her first year of using birth control.[37] That's why even Planned Parenthood's research institute had to admit that most high school pregnancies are caused by contraceptive failure, not by the failure to use them.[38] Now, consider that a woman can get pregnant only a few days of the month—but you can get an STD any day.
- Birth-control pills interfere with a woman's immune system,[39] making her more likely to contract certain STDs.[40] Among countless other side effects, the pill increases a woman's chance of having breast cancer,[41] cervical cancer,[42] liver cancer,[43] and potentially fatal blood clots.[44]
- The shot (Depo-Provera) and the patch (Ortho Evra) carry similar risks, or worse.[45] That's why the makers of the patch are facing lawsuits related

to deaths and other injuries from thousands of women.[46] Meanwhile, women have sued the makers of the shot for 700 million dollars![47] One reason for this is because the shot thins out a woman's bones.[48] This is especially worrisome for young women, because the teenage years are a critical time for bone development. After years of receiving birth control injections as a teen, a girl in her early 20's could have the bones of a 50 to 60 year old. Interestingly, because of its link to breast cancer, veterinarians stopped prescribing Depo-Provera for dogs.[49] However, it's still being given to women, and is sometimes injected into male sex offenders as a punishment that decreases their sex drive![50]

- When birth control fails, many are offered abortion as a solution, and are told that their life will return to normal after the procedure. However, such women often experience depression, and are six times more likely to commit suicide than women who gave birth.[51]

These statistics are not listed in order to frighten you. Instead, they've been included so that you will be better able to love. By practicing chastity, *you not only protect yourself, you protect your future spouse and children if you do get married.*

If you've been sexually active, go get tested. Don't put this off because of fear. If the clinic offers you birth control, you can decline, because you have self-control.

You might wonder, "If I can't use a condom, then how am I supposed to protect myself?" For one, *you can know it isn't love if you feel the need to protect yourself from your beloved.* You protect yourself from enemies. You receive your beloved without reserve. If you aren't married and ready to receive that person fully, then it's not time to give him or her your body. We weren't designed to be given in pieces.

Even if we don't want it to, sex creates a long-lasting bond. This is because the gift of sexuality is meant for a greater purpose than passing relationships. With one sexual act, a child can be created. That's how tremendous the act of lovemaking is. The act cries out for permanence. By his or her existence, that child is saying, "I'm permanent, so you two should be as well!"

Often, the couple knows they're not ready for the total giving and commitment their act is saying, so they deny the natural process of life-giving love. They treat pregnancy as a disease against which they must be protected or vaccinated, instead of a gift to receive with joy.

"What if I'm sexually active now?"

Stop the sexual activity, and consider if you're a better person because of the relationship. Or, is it turning you into someone you never wanted to be? Don't remain in the relationship to be a hero or to rescue the other person. You'll only end up getting hurt. You might need to break up, but at least take some time away. If the person loves you, he or she will give you as much time and space as you need. And if this is real love, then taking a break won't hurt.

Ask yourself, "Is my boyfriend (or girlfriend) saying, 'I won't wait for you. If you love me you'd sleep with me now'? Or, 'I want the best for you, and I know our love is strong enough to save that gift until marriage'?" If your date won't do what's best for you before marriage, don't expect things to change in marriage. *You won't miss out on love if you leave a dead-end relationship.* The only way you'll miss out on love is if you stay, blindly hoping that things will miraculously improve.

Instead, make a firm decision, as this sixteen-year-old did: "No more baggage, no alcohol, no drugs, no excuses, no hasty rationalizations, no lies, just pure love. I think that's what I've been looking for this whole time." So, make this decision for yourself, and don't settle for anything less than real love.

"How do I say 'no'?"

If you want love, then the most important word you need to learn is *no*. By saying no to the cheap imitations of love, you're saying yes to the real thing. When you need to draw the line, be clear, confident, and firm. Be sure to say "no" with your words and your body language. If you are lying on a couch with your date and whispering a half-hearted "no," he or she probably won't take you seriously, since you don't take yourself seriously.

If your heart says, "Maybe I shouldn't be doing this," listen to that intuition and get out of the situation. How? Any way that will work: say that you respect the other person too much to do that with him or her. Or, say that you don't feel comfortable, that you need to get home, or blame it on your parents. I heard of one girl who said to her date, "Here's my cell phone. Call my dad, and if he says it's okay, then I'm ready." Better yet, say that only your future spouse deserves to get that close to you, and then only after you're married. Most of all, don't be afraid to look a person in the eye and say, "no." If you freely give your body to others, it commands no respect because there's dullness in a person who is unable to set standards and have the character to stick to them. On the other hand, people commit for life to those who respect themselves.

If you want to avoid hurting the other's feelings, compliment him or her on why you enjoy being together. Then, explain how purity unites a couple better than passion. This shows that you aren't pushing him or her away, but are seeking a deeper love. But realize that you don't owe your date a thirty-minute lecture on why chastity is important to you. If your date loves you, then he or she won't pressure you. This is the real test to see if you are being loved or used. "Love waits to give, but lust can't wait to get."[52]

"How do I avoid mistakes in the future?"

Avoid situations where mistakes often happen, such as being alone together at home, in the back room of a party, or on a bed. The situation may seem harmless, but can result in something as serious as date rape. Avoid drugs and alcohol, which are the gateway to many regrets. These can influence you to do things that you would otherwise reject. Some people use them for just this reason: so that they can blame the substances for their own behavior.

It's one thing to avoid a bad situation, and it's another to avoid a bad relationship. So take time to build a friendship first. Know your standards and make sure your date not only respects them, but shares them, too. Don't pursue a relationship with a person who wears down your morals and will physically take from you everything that you're willing to give. You deserve better. Another wise move is to date only someone you can see yourself marrying. If we get involved in relationships that we know won't last, we're training ourselves for divorce.

Now, I'd like to say a word to young women hoping for love. This may not be fun to hear, but keep in mind

I say this as a guy in my twenties: During your teenage years, stay away from older guys.

Here's why: 74 percent of girls who lose their virginity as teens lose it to an older guy.[53] In fact, the majority of teen pregnancies are caused by older guys.[54] Why do so many young women fall into this trap? One reason is because girls mature sooner than boys do. A teenage girl may be bored with the maturity level of guys her own age. Older guys realize this, and have more refined "grooming techniques" to flatter girls by the attention. For example, he may give her a promise ring and tell her they'll be together forever, so that she'll think any sexual activity they share is more special. Distractions like this quiet the girl's intuitions that are probably screaming at her to stay away from him.

Older guys also use lines like "I've never felt this way about a girl before . . . but I'm okay if *you* don't want to have sex." Some girls melt at hearing this because they think the guy really wants what's best for them. In reality, he probably doesn't have enough social skills to date a girl his own age, and he figures that a naive younger girl is less likely to have the maturity and confidence to turn him down. It's not the girl's job to be the "chastity cop," but a man will be as much of a gentleman as a woman requires. Obviously, not all older guys are bad, but if he's as good as you think he is, why hasn't a girl his own age snatched him up by now?

Also, ask yourself, "What is my body worth?" Is it for sale at the price of a movie and dinner? No matter how much a guy spends on the date, you're not obligated to offer him your body. Remember that anyone who breaks up with you because you don't give in to his lust isn't worthy of your attention to begin with.

A word for the guys: Don't wait for the girl to stop. A real man guards a woman's innocence instead of seeking ways to empty her of it. It's no coincidence that the word *virtue* comes from a Latin root meaning "manly strength." When a man practices the virtue of chastity, he becomes more masculine. According to one college woman, "Being able to have sex isn't what makes a boy into a man. Anyone can have sex. It's the ability to have self-control that sets the men apart from the boys." So, realize that *women seek purity in a man*, because purity is a requirement of love.

"Does how I dress make a difference in how a guy treats me?"

Women deserve unconditional respect no matter what they wear. However, the way a girl dresses (and dances) sends a message to men. If her sexual value is the first impression she gives to a man, she'll be more likely to encounter the type of guys who want to use her body. They might say or do whatever is necessary to get access to it. But, after she gives in, they often lose respect for her, get bored, and leave. Meanwhile, she's left thinking, "Maybe if I had been skinnier, or had done more with him sexually, he would have liked me more and stayed longer." No, but he may have used her longer. The ultimate cause of this was not her outfit, but rather the failure of the man and the woman to treat each other with love. But if a woman yearns to be treated with such reverence, then she cannot afford to forget that she has power in the way she presents herself to men.

Modesty is a bold statement of your worth because it invites men to consider something deeper about you. It tells a guy that he can take you seriously as a woman, because you don't need to make boys gawk at you in order to feel secure. I'll grant that guys will stare at a girl who wears a short skirt that could be mistaken for a wide belt. But none of them respect her more because of it. As a woman, do you long to be simply gawked at, or to be loved?

If your heart is saying, "Is this too short?" or "Is this too tight?" listen to that intuition because it answered your question. Stand in front of a mirror and ask, "What am I drawing attention to with this outfit? Is this outfit saying that the best thing about me is my body, or does it announce that I'm worth waiting to see?"

Modesty does not mean that you look unattractive or cover every inch of your body as if it's bad or dirty. Like a bride wearing a veil, clothing conceals a woman's body as an invitation of respect. You deserve to be treated with reverence—not like a collection of body parts. But if you don't realize your own dignity, how will a man?

A woman's most fascinating trait is the mystery of her femininity. Men find it captivating, and it is something to guard at all costs. Modesty preserves this mystery, since *nothing adorns a woman with as much beauty as purity does.* Modest dress manifests pure womanhood, and this is the first line of defense for the virtue of chastity. So realize that purity is attractive. After all, you're not *playing* hard to get—you *are* hard to get.

"If a guy has a bad imagination, isn't that his problem?"

It is his problem. But when a woman gets frustrated because men don't respect her, it becomes her problem, too. That's why modesty is called the guardian of love. When a guy meets a woman who respects herself, he knows that if he wants to enjoy her company, he'll need to be a gentleman.

If you want to find a man of character, realize that they aren't looking for a girl who dresses provocatively. Unfortunately, the media tells women that the less they wear, the more guys will like them. Girls are also led to believe that their bodies are never perfect enough, and that if they want love, they have to look like the starving airbrushed models in fashion magazines (who, by the way, never seem to have perfect relationships). When a girl focuses so much on the physical aspect, she may overlook what qualities a virtuous guy would hope to find in her: faithfulness, honesty, and respect.

You may be thinking, "That sounds great, but where are these ideal men hiding?" Well, I've met plenty of young guys who wonder the same thing about modest women. It's almost as if we're so concerned about what others think that we're too afraid to be ourselves. We become so obsessed with the opinions of others that we ignore the desires of our own hearts.

Most women don't dress to incite lustful thoughts. If anything, they're more concerned about what other women will think of their outfit! However, a woman who desires love shoots herself in the foot if she dresses immodestly. She may think that her outfit is cute, but trust me—he's not looking at her outfit. Instead, his lust is causing him to become a slave to his weakness. Even though men generally don't like to ask for help, when it comes to having a pure mind, we need the help of women. Men need to be taught how to love in a noble way, and educated that women have a value that far exceeds the beauty of their bodies.

Some women are so busy trying to turn a guy's head that they never realize they have the power to turn a guy's heart. Girls, *do not underestimate your power to change the way the world looks at sex and the dignity of womanhood.*

"How do I stay pure?"

First of all, don't let the fear of rejection control your relationships. Many young women are afraid of offending or losing their boyfriends if they don't yield to their sexual demands. One woman said, "So often girls think, 'I have to do it to please him,' but later they feel awful, particularly when he runs off with another girl."[55] These insecurities must be overcome if you are ever to be loved as you deserve. Instead of worrying about him leaving if you don't give him something sexual, let him worry about *you* leaving unless he respects you!

Similarly, many guys are afraid that a girl will think less of them if they turn down her sexual advances. But if a girl is pressuring you, it might be because she is afraid you will ignore or reject her if she doesn't offer you something sexual.

Besides guarding your body, guard your mind as well. Don't warp your imagination with sensual TV shows, websites, movies, magazines, gossip, or music that glorifies meaningless sex. Some people justify their enjoyment of these by saying that they're not affected. This is like thinking you won't be stained by rolling in tar. If you are serious about love, get rid of these things. Ask yourself: "Is it that I couldn't be trying any more to avoid lust, or that I couldn't be trying any less?"

"As a guy, isn't having a pure mind impossible?"

Having sexual desires isn't bad. It's normal. But we must control our imagination, cleanse our speech, and avoid looking at girls as objects. There's a battle between love and lust in all of us. But, by becoming pure gentlemen, we'll conquer temptations and learn to love women instead of using them.

If you've ever wrestled, you know that where you direct your opponent's head his body will follow. The same is true of your mind. Control your sexual thoughts, and you will gain discipline over your body.

The more you practice chastity, the easier it becomes, and the better you'll prepare yourself for love. For example, when men are pure, they learn how to show true love and affection. A man becomes a better lover since he learns to love the whole woman, not just her body. Therefore, chastity is not the absence of temptation, but the victory of love over it.

This is why the need for chastity does not end when you get married. Chastity is the capacity to love another and have respect for the gift of sexuality, no matter what your state in life: married or single. So, while abstinence ends for couples who marry, chastity holds them together. If you're sick of divorce and you hope that if you do get married that it will last, start living the virtue of chastity today.

"What do I do now?"

Don't be passive, but prepare for real love. One way to do this is to enjoy being single. Most teens are under such pressure to constantly have a boyfriend or girlfriend that they never have the time or space to discover their own identity and dreams. Or, they feel as if there is something defective about them because they are not in a relationship. Don't fall for this. As one high school girl said to me, "You don't go through high school looking for your husband. You go through high school looking for your bridesmaids." Follow her advice, and hang out with friends who support your lifestyle instead of wearing it down.

In your relationships, set your standards high, because you'll get what you'll settle for. If you need to lower them to date someone, something is wrong. So, write down the standards that you hope for your spouse to meet. After writing the list, read it and ask yourself: "By the way I'm living today, do I deserve this person?" If not, begin to become the one who does. Even if you have no plans of marriage, you will not regret this decision to respect yourself.

Some of the best things in life are obtained through trial and suffering. Sacrifice and self-denial are necessary if a person wishes to build love. But do not be afraid when love makes demands on you, because you deserve such love—and you will not be satisfied with anything less. If you want love to be as good as it gets, you must persevere. Lust promises everything, but gives nothing. Love promises a difficult path, but will give you more than you ever imagined. You have nothing to lose, everything to gain, and will have no more regrets. *Purity knows no regrets.*

In an age in which people expect instant gratification, chastity proclaims a challenge of sacrifice and patience. It's a battle. But know that this purity of mind, heart, and body is possible. As a twenty-seven-year-old virgin engaged to the woman whose quote is on page 16, I know it is possible—and well worth it!

1 S. Ryan, et al., "The First Time: Characteristics of Teens' First Sexual Relationships," *Research Brief* (Washington, D.C.: Child Trends, August, 2003), 5.

2 Josh McDowell and Dick Day, *Why Wait: What You Need to Know about the Teen Sexuality Crisis* (San Bernardino, Calif.: Here's Life Publishers, 1987).

3 Meg Meeker, M.D., *Epidemic: How Teen Sex Is Killing Our Kids* (Washington, D.C.: Lifeline Press, 2002), 78.

4 Carmichael, et al., "Plasma oxytocin increases in the human sexual response," *The Journal of Clinical Endocrinology and Metabolism* 64:1 (January 1987): 27–31; Murphy, et al., "Changes in oxytocin and vasopressin secretion during sexual activity in men," *The Journal of Clinical Endocrinology and Metabolism* 65:4 (October 1987): 738–741.

5 Kosfeld, et al., "Oxytocin increases trust in humans," *Nature* 435 (2005): 673–676; Heinrichs, et al., "Selective amnesic effects of oxytocin on human memory," *Physiology & Behavior* 83 (2004): 31–38; Bartz, et al., "The neuroscience of affiliation: Forging links between basic and clinical research on neuropeptides and social behavior," *Hormones and Behavior* 50 (2006): 518–528; B. Ditzen, "Effects of Social Support and Oxytocin on Psychological and Physiological Stress Responses during Marital Conflict," International Congress Of Neuroendocrinology, Pittsburgh, PA: 19–22 June 2006; Crenshaw, M.D., *The Alchemy of Love and Lust* (New York: Pocket Books, 1996); Louann Brizendine, *The Female Brain* (New York: Morgan Road Books, 2006), 65–74.

6 E. Svoboda, "Inhaled 'Cuddle' Hormone Promotes Trust," *Discover* 27:1 (January 2006): 56.

7 Bartels and Zeki, "The neural correlates of maternal and romantic love," *NeuroImage* 21 (2004): 1155–1166.

8 Cf. Pfaff, et al., "Neural Oxytocinergic Systems as Genomic Targets for Hormones and as Modulators of Hormone-Dependant Behaviors," *Results and Problems in Cell Differentiation* 26 (1999): 91–105, as quoted by Eric J. Keroack, M.D., and John R. Diggs, Jr., M.D., "Bonding Imperative," A Special Report from the Abstinence

Medical Council (Abstinence Clearinghouse, 30 April 2001); K. Joyner and R. Udry, "You Don't Bring Me Anything but Down: Adolescent Romance and Depression," *Journal of Health and Social Behavior* 41:4 (December 2000):361–391; Hallfors, et al., "Which Comes First in Adolescence—Sex and Drugs or Depression?" *American Journal of Preventive Medicine* 29:3 (2005): 163–170.

9   Edward O. Laumann, et al., *The Social Organization of Sexuality: Sexual Practices in the United States* (Chicago: University of Chicago Press, 1994), 503.

10 R. Finger, et al., "Association of Virginity at Age 18 with Educational, Economic, Social, and Health Outcomes in Middle Adulthood," *Adolescent & Family Health* 3:4 (2004): 169.

11 Cf. Bennett, et. al., "Commitment and the Modern Union: Assessing the Link Between Premarital Cohabitation and Subsequent Marital Stability," *American Sociological Review* 53:1 (February 1988): 127–138.

12 Forste, et al., "Sexual Exclusivity Among Dating, Cohabiting, and Married Women," *Journal of Marriage and the Family* 58:1 (1996): 43.

13 Centers for Disease Control, "Youth Risk Behavior Surveillance — United States, 2005," *Morbidity and Mortality Weekly Report* 55:SS-5 (9 June 2006): 19.

14 Cf. Centers for Disease Control, "Trends in HIV-Related Behaviors Among High School Students — United States 1991–2005," *Morbidity and Mortality Weekly* 55:31 (11 August 2006): 851–854.

15 National Campaign to Prevent Teen Pregnancy, *America's Adults and Teens Sound Off About Teen Pregnancy: An Annual National Survey* (16 December 2003), 17.

16 Philip Rivers, *A Winning Lifestyle with Philip Rivers* (DVD), Diocese of San Diego, 2007.

17 Foundation for the Family, *Practicing Teen Chastity* (Cincinnati, OH.: Couple to Couple League).

18 "True to His Word" abcnews.com, 29 October 2002.

19 Cf. William R. Mattox, Jr., "Aha! Call it the revenge of the church ladies," *USA TODAY*, 11 February 1999, 15-A.

20 Cf. William R. Mattox Jr., "The Hottest Valentines: the Startling

Secret of What Makes You a High-Voltage Lover," *The Washington Post,* 13 February 1994.

21 Dawn Eden, *The Thrill of the Chaste* (Nashville, T.N.: W Publishing Group, 2006), xii.

22 Christopher West, *Good News about Sex and Marriage* (Ann Arbor, Mich.: Charis Books, 2000), 84.

23 Cf. Martinon-Torres, et al., "Human papillomavirus vaccines: A new challenge for pediatricians," *Anales de Pediatría* 65:5 (November 2006): 461–469; Trottier, et al., "The epidemiology of genital human papillomavirus infection,"*Vaccine* 24:S1 (March 2006): 4; Division of STD Prevention "Prevention of Genital HPV Infection and Sequelae: Report of an External Consultants' Meeting," Department of Health and Human Services, Atlanta: Centers for Disease Control and Prevention (CDC) (December 1999): 1.

24 Cf. J. M. Walboomers, et al., "Human Papillomavirus Is a Necessary Cause of Invasive Cervical Cancer Worldwide," *Journal of Pathology* 189:1 (September 1999): 12–19.

25 World Health Organization, International Agency for Research on Cancer, 2006 (www.iarc.fr).

26 Cf. National Institutes of Health, "Scientific Evidence on Condom Effectiveness for Sexually Transmitted Disease (STD) Prevention" (June 2000), 26. (www.niaid.nih.gov/dmid/stds/condomreport.pdf); House of Representatives, "Breast and Cervical Cancer Prevention and Treatment Act of 1999," 22 November 1999.

27 Division of STD Prevention, "Prevention of Genital HPV Infection and Sequelae: Report of an External Consultants' Meeting," 7.

28 Cf. Bearman, et al., "Chains of Affection: The Structure of Adolescent Romantic and Sexual Networks," *American Journal of Sociology* 110:1 (2004): 44–91.

29 Joe McIlhaney, M.D., *Safe Sex* (Grand Rapids, Mich.: Baker Book House, 1991), 23.

30 Cf. Medical Institute for Sexual Health, *Sex, Condoms, and STDs: What We Now Know* (Austin, Tex.: Medical Institute for Sexual Health, 2002); B. Dillion, "Primary HIV Infections Associated with

Oral Transmission," CDC's 7th Conference on Retroviruses and Opportunistic Infections, Abstract 473, San Francisco, February 2000; Centers for Disease Control, "Transmission of Primary and Secondary Syphilis by Oral Sex – Chicago, Illinois, 1998–2002," *Morbidity and Mortality Weekly Report* 51:41 (22 October 2004): 966–968.

31 Cf. C. Sonnex, et al., "Detection of Human Papillomavirus DNA on the Fingers of Patients with Genital Warts," *Sexually Transmitted Infections* 75 (1999): 317–319; Winer, et al., "Genital Human Papillomavirus Infection: Incidence and Risk Factors in a Cohort of Female University Students," *American Journal of Epidemiology* 157:3 (2003): 218–226; Tabrizi, et al., "Prevalence of Gardnerella vaginalis and Atopobium vaginae in virginal women," *Sexually Transmitted Diseases* 33:11 (November 2006): 663–665.

32 Cf. Ley, et al., "Determinants of Genital Human Papillomavirus Infection in Young Women," *Journal of the National Cancer Institute* 83:14 (July 1991): 997–1003.

33 Cf. Hammarstedt, et al., "Human papillomavirus as a risk factor for the increase in incidence of tonsillar cancer," *International Journal of Cancer* 119:11 (December 2006): 2620–2623.

34 Centers for Disease Control, "Tracking the Hidden Epidemics, Trends in STDs in the United States 2000," (6 April 2001), 6.

35 Cf. P. Leone, "Type-specific Serologic Testing for Herpes Simplex Virus-2," *Current Infectious Disease Reports* 5:2 (April 2003):159–165.

36 Cf. Bosch, et al., "Male Sexual Behavior and Human Papillomavirus DNA: Key Risk Factors for Cervical Cancer in Spain," *Journal of the National Cancer Institute* 88:15 (August 1996): 1060–1067.

37 Haishan Fu, et al., "Contraceptive Failure Rates: New Estimates From the 1995 National Survey of Family Growth," *Family Planning Perspectives* 31:2 (March/April 1999): 61.

38 Santelli, et al., "Contraceptive Use and Pregnancy Risk Among U.S. High School Students, 1991–2003," *Perspectives on Sexual and Reproductive Health* 38:2 (June 2006): 109.

39 Cf. Yovel, et al., "The Effects of Sex, Menstrual Cycle, and Oral Contraceptives on the Number and Activity of Natural Killer

Cells," *Gynecologic Oncology* 81:2 (May 2001): 254–262; Blum, et al.,
"Antisperm Antibodies in Young Oral Contraceptive Users," *Advances
in Contraception* 5 (1989): 41–46; Critchlow, et al., "Determinants
of cervical ectopia and of cervicitis: age, oral contraception, specific
cervical infection, smoking, and douching," *American Journal of
Obstetrics and Gynecology* 173:2 (August 1995): 534–43.

40 Cf. Baeten, et al., Hormonal contraception and risk of sexually
transmitted disease acquisition: results from a prospective study,"
American Journal of Obstetrics and Gynecology 185:2 (August
2001): 380–385; Ley, et al., "Determinants of Genital Human
Papillomavirus Infection in Young Women," *Journal of the National
Cancer Institute* 83:14 (July 1991): 997–1003; Prakash, et al., "Oral
contraceptive use induces upregulation of the CCR5 chemokine
receptor on CD4(+) T cells in the cervical epithelium of healthy
women," *Journal of Reproductive Immunology* 54 (March 2002):
117–131; Wang, et al., "Risk of HIV infection in oral contraceptive
pill users: a meta-analysis," *Journal of Acquired Immune Deficiency
Syndromes* 21:1 (May 1999): 51–58; Lavreys, et al., "Hormonal contraception and risk of HIV-1 acquisition: results from a 10-year prospective study," *AIDS* 18:4 (March 2004): 695–697.

41 Cf. Chris Kahlenborn, MD, et al., "Oral Contraceptive Use as a Risk
Factor for Premenopausal Breast Cancer: A Meta-analysis," *Mayo
Clinic Proceedings* 81:10 (October 2006): 1290–1302; Collaborative
Group on Hormonal Factors in Breast Cancer, "Breast cancer and
hormonal contraceptives: collaborative reanalysis of individual data
on 53,297 women with breast cancer and 100,239 women without
breast cancer from 54 epidemiological studies," *Lancet* 347 (June
1996): 1713–1727; World Health Organization, "IARC Monographs
Programme Finds Combined Estrogen-Progestogen Contraceptives
and Menopausal Therapy are Carcinogenic to Humans," International
Agency for Research on Cancer, Press Release 167 (29 July 2005).

42 Cf. Smith, et al., "Cervical cancer and use of hormonal contraceptives: A systematic review," *Lancet* 361 (2003):1159–1167.

43 Cf. World Health Organization, "IARC Monographs Programme

Finds Combined Estrogen-Progestogen Contraceptives and Menopausal Therapy are Carcinogenic to Humans," International Agency for Research on Cancer, Press Release 167 (29 July 2005); La Vecchia, "Oral contraceptives and cancer," *Minerva Ginecologica* 58:3 (June 2006): 209–214.

44 Cf. *Physicians' Desk Reference*, 2415; Kemmeren, et al., "Third generation oral contraceptives and risk of venous thrombosis: meta analysis," *British Medical Journal* 323 (July 2001): 131–134; Parkin, et al., "Oral contraceptives and fatal pulmonary embolism," *The Lancet* 355:9221 (June 2000): 2133–2134; Hedenmalm, et al., "Fatal venous thromboembolism associated with different combined oral contraceptives," *Drug Safety* 28:10 (2005): 907–916; Sameuelsson, et al., "Mortality from venous thromboembolism in young Swedish women and its relation to pregnancy and use of oral contraceptives," *European Journal of Epidemiology* 20:6 (2005): 509–516.

45 Cf. Physicians' Desk Reference, 2409, 2620–2621; Morrison, et al., "Hormonal Contraceptive Use, Cervical Ectopy, and the Acquisition of Cervical Infections," *Sexually Transmitted Diseases* 31:9 (September 2004): 561–567; U.S Food and Drug Administration, "Ortho Evra (norelgestromin/ethinyl estradiol) Information," Department of Health and Human Services (20 September 2006).

46 Johnson & Johnson, SEC Filing, Annual Report for Period Ended 9/30/07; Associated Press, "Birth control patch linked to higher fatality rate," 20 July 2005.

47 CTV.ca News, "Class action suit filed over birth control drug," (19 December 2005).

48 U.S. Food and Drug Administration, "Black Box Warning Added Concerning Long-Term Use of Depo-Provera Contraceptive Injection," FDA Talk Paper (17 November 2004).

49 "The Case Against Depo-Provera: Problems in the U.S.," *Multinational Monitor* 6:2–3 (February/March 1985); Depo-Provera, Patient Labeling, Pharmacia & Upjohn Company (October 2004).

50 Cf. T.A. Kiersch, "Treatment of sex offenders with Depo-Provera," *The Bulletin of the American Academy of Psychiatry and the Law*

18:2 (1990): 179–187; Assembly Bill 3339, "An act to repeal and add Section 645 of the Penal Code, relating to crimes," California State Senate, Amended 20 August 1996; 2005; California Penal Code, 645.

51 Cf. Fergusson, et al., "Abortion in young women and subsequent mental health," *Journal of Child Psychology and Psychiatry* 47:1 (January 2006): 16–24; Gissler, et al., "Suicides after pregnancy in Finland, 1987–1994: register linkage study," *British Medical Journal* 313 (December 1996): 1431–1434.

52 Cloud and Townsend, *Boundaries in Dating* (Mich.: Zondervan Publishing House, 2000), 251.

53 Ryan, et al., "The First Time: Characteristics of Teens' First Sexual Relationships," 2.

54 Cf. Hsu G., "Statutory Rape: The dirty secret behind teen sex numbers," *Family Policy* (1996): 1–16.

55 Foundation for the Family, *Practicing Teen Chastity*, Cincinnati, Ohio.

THE SEXUAL CULTURE WAR IS ON

SEXTING, FACEBOOK GOSSIP, PORNOGRAPHY, HOOKING UP, BROKEN FAMILIES, AND BROKEN HEARTS.

HOW DO YOU TURN PEER PRESSURE INTO PURE PRESSURE?

Jason and Crystalina Evert have spoken to more than one million teens on five continents. Now, schedule a presentation to have them inspire the youth in your junior high, high school, university, or conference.

Teens today need straight answers to tough questions about dating, relationships, and sexual purity. That's why Chastity Project offers more than a dozen presentations designed to empower students and parents.

FOR MORE INFORMATION, VISIT